Fashion Victims:

Missing Style by a

Marvelous Mile

By

Linda Ann Nickerson

Gait
House
Press

Published in the United States by Gait House Press.

Printed in the United States of America.

2021

Cover and internal illustration/s:

Public domain photo

Fashion Victims: Missing Style by a Marvelous Mile

By

Linda Ann Nickerson

Dedication

Fashion Victims: Missing Style by a Marvelous Mile is dedicated to more than a few favorite fabulously frumpy friends, who could not care one whit what style mavens may say about what they wear or the way they look.

By the way, I think you look fabulous. Every one of you.

Contents

Introduction 11

A-Tired: A Limericked Toil to Prevent Sad Spoil 17

The Bare Truth: A Crazy Conjunction on Wardrobe
Malfunction 19

Tracking the Wherewithal: A Tale of Paces and Looser
Laces 20

Glasses of Rose: A Change of View May Simply Do .. 22

Bell Curve: Limerick Cries Right Before Your Eyes ... 24

Shoes to Schmooze: Secrets to Stepping into Sentiment
with Style 25

Just a Jersey: Easy Shreds on Favorite Threads 26

Oh, No, Retro: Limericked Sway on Style Past Its Day
.... 27

Blingle Belles: True Triolets for My Merry Musettes .. 28

Fashion Affront: When Forth to Back Are Out of Whack
.... 32

Compassion for Fashion: An Ode to Vogue's Victims. 34

Style to Boot: A Bounding Bill for Footwear Frill 36

Clothes Hoarse: When Focus Fogs with Talk of Togs.. 37

Denim Deluxe: Revisiting Rants on a Shared Pair of Pants 39

Solar Flare: Peek Oblique at Season's Shriek..............41

Dress Up or 'Fess Up: Some Lines to Yield a Youth Concealed 42

Ego Drip: A Melodic Brush with Unreturned Crush 43

Kickin' It: Step by Step with Perky Pep 45

Strut Not to Wear: Nonet and Couplet for the Style Set 46

Epicure and Couture: Metered Lines on One Who Dines 47

You Schmooze, You Lose: Pandemic Blues.................49

Suits and Pursuits: A Trace to Warn Those Who Adorn 51

Fair Warning: A Poetic Tense on Style Sense 53

Dressed-Up Dregs: A Few Lines Forlorn, As the Gown Must Be Worn..55

False Start at the Mega-Mart: A Story in Song on a Store That's Gone Wrong 56

Coming Clean: When Seasons' Styles Are Stowed Awhile 60

Garbled Style for a While: When Fashion's Vault Leads to Default 62

Straightening Up: Setting Things Right When Life Takes a Bite 65

Greenback Attack: Poetic Sighs on Finding a Prize 66

Hanging by a Hair: Scuttlebutt on Making the Cut.......68

The Unreal Ideal: When Such a Bod Deserves No Nod 69

Hey, Supermodel: A Rhyme from the Mind of a Man Most Unkind 71

Hues to Amuse: Creative Flows on Cheery Clothes 73

Don't Smile at Me That Way: A Rhyming Spin on the Inverted Grin...74

Idols and Icons: A Cinquain Form Debating Norm 76

Comfort Clothes: Strands in the Sands 77

Lipschtick: Simple Lines on Smile of Wine 79

Dandies on Display: A Gussied Verse to Break the Purse 80

Loads of Laundry: Acrostic Posh on Doing Wash.......81

Pinata Sonata: Swinging Toy on Party Boy.................82

The Mirror Lied: A Rhyming Write on Altered Sight ..84

Reach for the Beach: A Limericked Run on a Form That Needs Sun 88

More, More: A Ballyhoo to Overdo 90

Out of Gases and Sunglasses: Making Peace with Price Increase 92

Quality Quit: Saving Chips as Style Slips 94

Shopping Sense: A Simple Spray on Scents at Play 96

Spandex and the Ex: Stylistic Throws as Family Grows 98

Stopping Shoe Shopping: A Loose-Laced Chuckle, So I Won't Buckle 100

Blooper-Vision: A Shiny Stint on Missing Tint 103

Stud, Sweat and Smears: When Being Brawn Is Overdrawn 105

Coif Duty: Tangled Talks on Ravaged Locks 106

Style Revival: A Rhyming Passion for Lasting Fashion 108

Unraveling: Nothing's As It Seams 111

Swimwear Is Life: A Rhymed Retort on Suits We Sport 113

Titled, But Unbridled: A Rhythmic Reel on a Royal Ideal 116

The Woes of Just-So's: Wrestling in Verse for Better or Worse...118

Mirror, Mirror: A Simple Squawk on Taking Stock...120

Worn Out Without a Doubt: Poetic Talk on Taking Stock 122

No Worse for Wear: A Patterned Wheel, Life to Reveal 124

About the author 129

"When I get a little money, I buy books; and if any is left, I buy food and clothes."

Desiderius Erasmus
Dutch Philosopher
(1466-1536)

Introduction

Fashion victims may cause others to cringe, but we can also celebrate a curious sort of victory.

We can all be fashion victims.

It's a fair bet we all have been victimized by fashion, at least once or twice. Fashion leads to foibles.

It's inevitable.

We miss the mark now and then, whether we mean to or not. Call it a bad hair day, a wardrobe malfunction, or just a funky get-up.

Maybe it even works.

I'd bet many wacky fashion trends started with goof-ups and gaffes. Take a look back at the torn-up jeans and ripped sweatshirt rages, if you don't believe me.

Hem and haw, if you will.

Fashion experts tell us style is king. Really?

That's the nature of modern modes, which fly at us with fads, tailor-made to call us to conformity. How often do we clothe our bodies, comb our hair, polish our nails, and coat our faces with whatever we perceive the current styles to be?

Perhaps the latest rages flatter us. Or perhaps not.

Do we care?

Some of us, whether daring or dowdy, will challenge such conventions. It can be cool to break a fashion rule.

When I was a teenager, for example, we buttoned woolen cardigan sweaters in the back on purpose. I can't even tell you why, but we did. We all did, even though most of us had hair so long that it covered our backs anyway.

We also wore headbands that were so tight that they actually hurt our heads.

And don't get me started on those old gym uniforms we sported daily. But then, we didn't exactly have a choice.

Not too long ago, my then-teens intentionally wore mismatched socks. That seemed to be the style. Before long, you could even purchase pairs of socks with stripes and patterns that didn't match. Maybe you still can.

Go figure, right?

It's all about fashion statements.

Perhaps it has always been so – at least since fig leaves entered the picture.

Some of our personal fashion victim stories can be the most comical memories life offers. Style is funny, especially when we take it too seriously. Sometimes it's downright hilarious.

What's more: Style can be a metaphor for living, whether we follow the patterns of current trends or not.

What does our attention (or lack of attention) to fashion say about our personalities or even our personal standards? How do our choices of apparel and accessories reveal who we are on the inside, or who we'd like to be?

What about personal grooming, hygiene, and ever-changing beauty trends and techniques?

This much is true: Some of us are simply happier with a little sand between our toes than with our feet stuffed into shiny shoes. We may or may not mind a bit of grime under our fingernails or a few tangles in our hair.

Maybe these less-than-fashionable traits make us a bit more grounded, even for a short spell.

Besides, we never know what we might step in or pick up at any moment.

Those who seem to slip through life seamlessly may be missing something special and unexpected along the way. Life's richest moments are never smooth as silk.

This poetry collection addresses such stories in various styles, including rhyme and meter, a few scraps of free verse, an assortment of acrostics, a smattering of literary techniques, and a measure of wry wrinkles.

Some poems are simple and straightforward, while other are strangely symbolic or even somewhat sarcastic.

Try these verses on for size.

More than a few phrasings will likely have you in stitches. Some may shock you with snarkiness or surprises.

I hope these pages won't put anyone's bloomers in a bundle. That's not my aim.

And please try not to identify any of the folks who

may have inspired some of these lines – especially the more laughable ones. No ill-will is intended.

Mostly, this is all for fun.

At the end of the line, I have to wonder whether we fashion victims may not be victims after all.

A-Tired: A Limericked Toil to Prevent Sad Spoil

My buttons are popping – who knows?
Ticked off from my head to my toes.
The list, it is long,
From here to Hong Kong,
And turns all my poems to prose.

To itemize ills would be wrong
And steal from my readers the song –
Suffice it to stay
It starts in foul play
With noses where they don't belong.

Though tempted the wrongs to expose,
Forgiveness and grace to foreclose,
My faith does appeal,
Lest joy they may steal,
And so I must don my mom clothes.

Apparel adult may be strong

And tailored for figures grown long.

Such garments I'll zip,

Perhaps, too, my lip,

For how many rights make a wrong?

I'll empty my wardrobe of woes

And pounce on the truth, I suppose.

Though facts may reveal

The sordid ordeal,

We fashion not what others chose.

The Bare Truth: A Crazy Conjunction on Wardrobe Malfunction

A man who owned only one suit

Went shoeless and sockless to boot.

When put on the spot,

He'd deem himself hot,

So ladies could not help but hoot!

"Hey, Bud. Happy birthday,"

    they roared,

To eye the sole suit he'd afford.

So all of Bud's days,

He'd shock and amaze.

Perhaps he was out of his gourd.

He celebrated his physique,

But others judged no winning streak.

Tracking the Wherewithal: A Tale of Paces and Looser Laces

She walks the mall for exercise
When sloppy stuff slips from the skies.
She doesn't shop
Or even stop.
Instead, she drops another size.

The teeming stores give her no stress,
Nor does the food court her obsess.
For what she wears,
She hardly cares
And places no demand on dress.

The clothes she sports,
    they matter not.
They fit.
They work.
They hit the spot.
And no one sees

Or disagrees,

Though their approval is unsought.

She grows more hardy every step,

Strides past each sale display with pep –

No need to buy

Or even try,

Unburdened by new stuff to schlep.

Her cheeks, they bear a rosy sheen.

Her pocketbook retains some green.

And she feels good

Around the 'hood.

She's lean, serene,

    and needs not preen.

Glasses of Rose: A Change of View May Simply Do

I'm looking at life
    through my glasses of rose.
Stepped out of the shell,
    wasting oceans of woes.
Still no one was able
    to disjoint my nose.
That merits some mention,
    for that's how it goes.

Ah, life is a beach,
    when we do what we chose.
And coasting or rowing,
    we face highs and lows.
Today's race is over.
    My toes, how they froze.
Adieu, off to rest,
    for I've earned my repose.

The light's at its close

    with a toast, I suppose.

For I'm looking at life

    through my glasses of rose.

Bell Curve: Limerick Cries Right
Before Your Eyes

My life has tossed to me a curve,

Far sooner than I should deserve.

A younger shape

Began to drape;

Dear Father Time,

     you've got some nerve!

My bathing suit has surely shrunk,

Much earlier than I'd have thunk.

The stretchy seam

Has sunk downstream

And put me in a summer funk.

This losing battle, through the years,

Reduces this adult to tears.

The bell curve calls,

As muscle falls,

And consummates my own worse fears.

Shoes to Schmooze: Secrets to Stepping into Sentiment with Style

We women, how we love our shoes –

With boots and flats and heels to choose.

Guys pick bouquets

To win our praise,

But fancy footwear starts our schmooze.

Although we love a single rose,

Forgo the lacy, racy clothes.

To earn our hearts,

Save Cupid's darts.

Sweet shoes will set us on our toes.

Just a Jersey: Easy Shreds on Favorite Threads

Just a jersey, tattered shirt,
Sporting streaks of paint and dirt –
Perfect pick.
Grab it quick.
Shed the stain of daily hurt.

Comfy clothes hold magic might,
Once we step from social sight.
Loosely togged,
We are unbogged.
At least, we feel thus overnight.

Oh, No, Retro: Limericked Sway on Style Past Its Day

There once was a fellow named Brad,

Most known for his penchant for plaid.

With argyle sock,

The catwalk he'd rock

In Grandfather's style gone bad.

For decades, folks eyed him askance,

Remarking on pleats in his pants.

Then vintage grew posh,

And wow. Oh, my gosh.

Old Brad became king of the dance.

Blingle Belles: True Triolets for My Merry Musettes

I've never been one
    to be bold with the bling.
A glittery glamour
    just isn't my thing.
But all bets are off
    when we line up to sing.

Alas, I digress.
        Do forgive me this part.
Perhaps the left corner's
    the best place to start.
A harmony surely
    has captured my heart.

It seems Princess Preppy
    has taken a turn.
The dearest of divas
    have helped me to learn.

And no more is casual
     my sole concern.

My sweatshirts and jeans
       have been my classic suits.
I've been on the run,
     sporting sneakers or boots.
It's really amazing
     I'm now in cahoots.

I've learned to love lipstick
     in each scarlet shade,
To polish my fingernails,
     uncoil my braid,
And sometimes to sing
     without being afraid.

These ladies crave sparkles
     and spangles and gold.
They rock out in silver
     and sequins, all told –
A spectacle surely

for all to behold.

No sweet matching blouses
        with collars starched down.
No billowing choir robes,
        making us drown.
Instead we go shiny,
        as we hit the town.

We strap on our heels,
        and we step on the stage.
We curl our eyelashes
        to sing off-the-page.
Beyond that, we party
        and act not our age.

It's true I have joined
        in the musical scene
To sing acapella
        and show off the sheen
With plentiful laughter
        and fun in-between.

But here is my secret,
  if fact be revealed:
This fellowship harmony
  has my heart healed.
I'd wear almost anything,
  if they appealed.

Fashion Affront: When Forth to Back
Are Out of Whack

She simply loves to exercise,
Despite the daunt of watching eyes.
In stretchy styles,
She logs her miles,
To trim her tummy, waist, and thighs.

Occasionally, she'll face flak;
Denizens of the gym do crack.
Each pant and grunt
May bring affront,
As gossips do their grit unpack.

She shrugs it off as never mind,
By fashion's forces not confined.
But one day's dress
Threatened distress
To see her britches' front behind.

She'd slipped them on while it was dark,
And somehow she had missed the mark.
The emblem clear
Was in the rear.
So onlookers sent up their snark.

She took the mishap all in stride,
And to her workout reapplied.
For she was fit;
No need to snit
And no skin spillage to deride.

Although her pants were in reverse,
She knew,
    for better or for worse,
True fashion's fools
Enforce the rules,
While athletes overlook the curse.

What matter is a simple gaffe,
If we but at ourselves can laugh?

Compassion for Fashion: An Ode to Vogue's Victims

I'd like to call up my compassion
For tragic victims of highest fashion.
Our young and old and in-between
Are sporting garb that's just obscene.

Those skimpy, stretchy, clingy tops
Are showing up in high-priced shops.
Torn jeans can fetch a price so dear,
They make your savings disappear.

And save those flip-flops for the shore;
They're not in style anymore.
Your chiropractor wants you back
Because your frozen arches crack.

Don't get me started on briefs or thongs;
Keep underwear where it belongs.
Don't wanna see your tidy whites,

So please respect our human rights.

Those baring midriffs, showing fat,

Are simply not where style is at.

Oh, pull your shirt down,

    honey please.

Your belly button's gonna freeze.

Strap on a belt, if you still can.

Pull up those pants, guy.

    Be a man.

When you sit down to rest awhile,

Don't flash us that inverted smile.

Dear fashion victims, hear the call:

Your styles are starting to appall.

We're giving you the 4-1-1.

Your exhibition days are done.

Style to Boot: A Bounding Bill for Footwear Frill

Her cowboy boots are smokin' hot,

The flashiest attire she's got.

Who knew red shoes

Could beat the blues

And attitude could be store-bought?

So kick 'em up,

    and let 'em shine.

'Dem boots are lookin' mighty fine.

Some saddle soap

Will light your lope.

Go do-si-do,

    and dance grapevine.

Clothes Hoarse: When Focus Fogs with Talk of Togs

She cuts a figure fine. It's true.
No hand-me-downs askance to view,
Nor dirty laundry out to air.
She simply speaks of things to wear.

Now, fashion's fun. And fashion's fine.
She talks about it all the time.
We'd almost say we can't believe
She wears her heart upon her sleeve.

A clearance sale sets her a-pant.
She'll hem and haw and rave and rant.
To strike a pose gives her no thought
In latest trends of style store-bought.

Before you tag me as a snitch,
I'll mention that she is a stitch.
No kid gloves needed with this one.

She's generally a load of fun.

Her company is pleasant, sure,
If clothing talk one can endure.
Although she dresses to the nines,
I'd bet my boots she never whines.

Well-heeled, she'd do an emperor proud,
Stand head and shoulders 'bove the crowd.
Her sentiments are sure, heartfelt.
She'd never hit below the belt.

But influence to spend she'll hold,
As she displays her card of gold.
When friends step out with her to shop,
Their pockets lighten 'fore they stop.

To cap things off, I have to say,
I'm having lunch with her today.
And if to browse we skip dessert,
I'll try hard not to lose my shirt.

Denim Deluxe: Revisiting Rants on a Shared Pair of Pants

If I were a seamstress

    with skills like my aunt's,

Adept with a needle and thread at a glance,

I'd stitch jeans so strong,

We'd pass them along,

And we could all fly

    by the seat of our pants.

I'd sew in some stretch,

    o the trousers would fit

My circle cf friends

    in the spots where they sit.

The large and the lean

And those in-between

Could wear them in turn,

    and the seams would not split.

These jeans through adventure

we gladly would wear,

In comedy, tragedy,

fashion, and flair.

We'd each take a turn

To linger and learn,

While wearing and airing a single sweet pair.

For what is a friendship,

lest favorites we share?

Solar Flare: Peek Oblique at Season's Shriek

A woman caught more than one stare,
While searching for ready-to-wear.
Her winter pale skin
Sent others a-spin,
With more than her soles yet to bare.

The fitting room curtain was slight.
It barely did shield her from sight.
The maillot revealed
A truth less concealed.
Her skin had not yet seen the light.

Dress Up or 'Fess Up: Some Lines to Yield a Youth Concealed

Sometimes I feel, or I suppose,
A little girl in grown-up clothes.
Not yet senescent,
  but of age,
I've stayed my soul at fresher stage.

If tailored, tasteful togs I wear,
I almost feel put-on for flair.
I'm happier in sneaks and jeans,
Such as I sported in my teens.

My kids may groan.
Their cohorts jeer,
But I refuse to overhear.
I'll never be the worse for wear,
If I can dress without a care.

Ego Drip: A Melodic Brush with Unreturned Crush

A love-smitten guy was irate
And worked himself into state.
He strutted and roared,
But still, she ignored –
His ego to under-inflate.

He fancied the belle of the ball,
But she refused for him to fall.
She turned on her heel,
Denied his appeal –
Perhaps 'twas not love after all.

A mirror may fib to convince
The lustiest lad he's a prince.
Such looks may deceive,
Or worse, misperceive.
Perhaps he may fetch just a wince.

The moral is clear nonetheless.

A way exists out of this mess.

When handsome hearts shine,

The homeliest find

That beauties may seek them to bless.

Kickin' It: Step by Step with Perky Pep

My brand-new kicks have style to suit.

They fit my feet with colors cute.

I hope they've springs

Or Hermes' wings

To trim my times in runs to boot.

Strut Not to Wear: Nonet and Couplet for the Style Set

Perfectly meticulous is he,

Always assiduously garbed.

Methodically he struts.

Deeply he bows to awe.

But is he joyful,

Dressing in-depth,

Or indeed

Mirror's

Fool?

Some folks dress just to impress.

Others try, but leave us to guess.

Epicure and Couture: Metered Lines on One Who Dines

Let's don our duds
    and do the town.
We'll hit the house
    and bring it down.
A price-less menu
    hints at class,
The waiter too,
    so be not crass.

Glance left and right;
    size up the joint.
Look 'round the crowd,
    but please don't point.
Your collar's crisp
    Your pleats are pressed.
And yet I find
    I'm blushing, stressed.

No algorithm
    makes it so,
No matter where
    you choose to go.
This much is true,
    he very least:
One can dress up
    and still be beast.

You Schmooze, You Lose: Pandemic Blues

The world's gone bonkers; there's no doubt.

We're closeted by those with clout.

We simply can't come out to play.

The virus has to go away

Because we cannot schmooze.

My muscles sag. My nerves, they knot.

My language, it has gone to pot.

I don't hold back a darn or heck.

The house is clean, but I'm a wreck

Because we cannot schmooze.

It's growing harder to assess

My errant need to underdress.

In leggings, PJs, sneaks and sweats,

I cruise the town with no regrets

Because we cannot schmooze.

We stare at screens to catch a glance
Of folks who can't see we've no pants.
We splurge on foods to snack in beds.
We're bleary eyed with pounding heads.
Because we cannot schmooze.

We want to wear our fancy clothes
And breathe fresh air with unmasked nose.
We want to push and shove and hug,
And yet we can't without a drug.
Because we cannot schmooze.

Get lost, Corona. Hit the bricks.
We're sick of science, politics.
We've had enough, and we don't care
Just get out of our uncut hair.
Because we cannot schmooze.

Pandemic life has no panache.
But will it come out in the wash?

Suits and Pursuits: A Trace to Warn Those Who Adorn

Accouterments can lend a hand
To button the career you've planned.
The costume you select to show
Displays far more than you may know.

A resume may serve you well,
Although it's difficult to tell.
The first impression you present
May you your pathway reinvent.

If you should sport disheveled 'do,
A saggy sock, unpolished shoe,
A faded knee or sloppy sleeve,
You may as well stand up and leave.

Appearances may not define
Your character or place in line.
Still, future bosses catch one glance.

Don't give them cause to look askance.

Just dress the part that you desire.
And chase the vision ever higher.
Never let them see you sweat,
And utter nothing you'll regret.

Fair Warning: A Poetic Tense on Style Sense

A young police force lives with me
And misdemeanor finds.
They point out fashion ills with glee,
This posse of designs.

My wardrobe is behind the time;
My children tell me so.
The clothes I wear
    commit a crime,
Most everywhere I go.

"No Trespassing."
       This sign they hold,
When I am getting dressed.
These deputies,
    though they be bold,
My closet, they arrest.

If children cannot tell the truth,
Then who else can I trust?
For they are innocent in youth,
As my attire they bust.

It's time to clear the closet out.
We're heading for the shops.
One thing is sure,
    without a doubt,
My kids are fashion cops.

Dressed-Up Dregs: A Few Lines Forlorn, As the Gown Must Be Worn

Deep in the pit of the pail,

She answered a fathomless wail.

Still needing a date,

Refusing to wait –

Alas, how her dreams did derail.

Already, she'd chosen a gown.

The calendar danced its countdown.

So, left home alone,

She picked up the phone

And offered to go with some clown.

Her escort to prom was a cad,

A truly despicable lad.

Despite his fine suit,

She gave him the boot

And danced with a sweet undergrad.

False Start at the Mega-Mart: A Story in Song on a Store That's Gone Wrong

Hey, whatever happened to customer service?
I stopped at the store,
> and may Heaven preserve us!
A quick trip transformed me into an ill mood,
With retailing rudeness and bad attitude.

I walked in the door,
> and a uniformed girl
Swerved a bevy of carts into me
> with a whirl.
"Hey, watch where you're going,"
> she snarled with a scowl.
Then she uttered a long stream
> of verbage most foul.

I wanted to turn
> and stomp out of the store,
But wondered,

"Would it be much better next door?"
And over the door
    flashed a neon so bright:
"In our place,
    the customer always is right."

I gathered my items
    and crossed off my list;
Asked a stocker for help,
    and he held up a fist.
My patience unwinding,
    I raced with my cart
To the least lengthy checker,
    Who seemed so street smart.

With four-inch-long talons,
    she dialed her phone
And started to gab
    in a zone all her own.
Behind me,
    a baby decided to wail,
As the chatty cashier

gnawed her long pinky nail.

Thus frustrated,
    glanced I at all of the rows,
Attempting to check out,
    or else come to blows.
Yet each of the registers
    offered no hope.
Oh, how was a shopper
    expected to cope?

A guy in line seven
    had broken a jar.
And a gal on eleven
    was simply bizarre.
But right in between them,
    cashier number ten
Was arguing prices
    with two older men.

At this point,
    clung to my last final nerve,

This surely was more

    than I'd come to deserve.

Then I heard a voice,

    through perhaps in my mind,"

"Need etiquette clean-up

    on aisle number nine."

Gee, next time I think I'll go shopping online.

Coming Clean: When Seasons' Styles Are Stowed Awhile

The clock is shifting.
>Months unwind.

It's time to leave the rest behind.
The snuffs that emanate from stuff
Must be removed.
>I've had enough.

In flowing force,
>I fill four crates

With fashions from my shifting weights.
I slide the boxes to the stairs.
Continuation?
>No one cares.

The rhythm of the season calls.
It's nearly time to deck the halls.
No pressure but my urge to sort;
Decluttering's Olympic sport.

Throw up the windows;

    catch a gust.

Arrange the knick-kracks.

    Kick up dust.

The vacuum sings its favorite keen.

C'mon, who says a whistle's clean?

Garbled Style for a While: When Fashion's Vault Leads to Default

This wardrobe needs an overhaul.
Perhaps a field trip to the mall.
Well, here's the gist:
My kids insist.
They're calling in a wrecking ball.

With dresses from the seventies
And other fashion felonies,
My style brings shame
Upon my frame.
It's time for new amenities.

Say, can you see pale jeans with bells,
The stonewashed skinnies,
    fond farewells?
Old cuffs and pleats,
Toss those receipts.
A road trip calls where whimsy dwells.

Don't get them started

    on the shoes –

The pointy toes, spike heels

    – bad news!

Oh, clogs, bewares!

How many pairs,

Are suffering from overuse?

My jungle

    – cluttered, hackneyed, spent –

Brings me to radical repent.

No wild fads,

Just classic adds.

To window-shop won't reinvent.

I shudder still

    with coins in hand.

If I had bills,

    I'd hold them fanned.

I do declare,

With pockets bare,

Such outings may be less than planned.

A change in vogue does me confound:
What if old fads come back around?

Straightening Up: Setting Things Right When Life Takes a Bite

My best friend just got braces,
    of course.
They went on the same week
    as her divorce.
Her story is gory,
    So I'll be discreet.
She's fixing her life
    And aligning her teeth.

She'll gnash them no more,
Since she showed him the door.
And her smile will be bright,
As she turns out all right.

Greenback Attack: Poetic Sighs on Finding a Prize

Last Monday, when I folded clothes
Straightway out of the wash, I froze.
A paper fluttered to the floor,
Right there, outside the bedroom door.

A lumpy, crusty sheet of white,
All clumped and tattered.
        What a sight.
I crouched upon the floor to reach
What cycled through the load with bleach.

Examining my find, I spied
George Washington upon one side.
But he had paled beyond recall,
Along with missing protocol.

The serial had turned to gray;
The legal tender rinsed away.

I flipped the note to look for green.
This dollar bill was scrubbed full-clean!

A pocket in some sharp capris
Had carried milk money with ease
Until a certain laundry stink
Had faded out the dollar's ink.

So sheepishly, I took the buck,
Up to the bank to try my luck.
The teller asked me with a grin,
"You laundered money, yet again?"

Hanging by a Hair: Scuttlebutt on Making the Cut

My mane is mindless, savage strew.
In short, these locks ain't got no clue.
Each tress does trickle, ne'er to tame,
With no smooth shine or form to frame.

My every fiber takes a stand;
Each filament flies out of hand.
I'd choose to charm these waves a-wild,
But they resist like wayward child.

I'm overdue (You may have guessed.)
To put the expert to the test.
So sign me up. I'll bring my mess
For wonder-working S-O-S.

The Unreal Ideal: When Such a Bod Deserves No Nod

Her figure is unreasonable;
No, she cannot be real.
Her tan is just unseasonable,
So why should it appeal?

That tiny waist,
    those mile-long limbs,
It simply isn't fair.
So top-heavy,
    she over-brims –
And picture-perfect hair!

We look upon her longingly,
With body-image guilt.
It isn't plastic surgery;
It's simply how she's built.

Who is this favorite flawless one,

The ideal for us all?
She was invented just for fun,
A child's fashion doll.

Hey, Supermodel: A Rhyme from the Mind of a Man Most Unkind

Miss model, you're so very tall.

There's not much to you, not at all.

You're positively underweight;

I'd bet that every month you're late.

If I should hug you, I'd get hurt

Because your bones stick through your shirt.

And when you swing that sassy bob,

You look just like a cotton swab.

"C'mon, baby. Dine with me.

Just another calorie.

One little bite, and you will see

That I can be your cup of tea."

So swirl and sway and swing and strut.

You work it, girl. You've got no butt.

But have a little ice cream coney.

71

Honey, you're just too darn boney.

Still, stroll the catwalk.
    Jump through hoops.
Live on liquids and runny soups.
Step over here in your shiny sheath.
My brother needs to pick his teeth.

Someday you'll grow strong and sturdy –
Maybe when you're over thirty.
And fashionistas will fade away,
As soon as your belly starts to sway.

Hues to Amuse: Creative Flows on Cheery Clothes

What colors can raise us from drab,

As artist his palette may dab?

Does violet cheer?

May red banish fear?

Can yellow transform blues to fab?

When grays drag our highlights away

And banish the brightest bouquet,

May rainbows appear

As moods chandelier

To turn frosty moods to sorbet.

Don't Smile at Me That Way: A Rhyming Spin on the Inverted Grin

We went out to the county fair,
And everyone in town was there –
With Ferris wheel,
    the rides that scare,
And junk-food hawkers everywhere.

But nothing there could quite torment
Or frighten me to the extent
As what I saw and did lament,
When we passed by the bingo tent.

Alas, here is my tale of woe:
The folks were seated in a row,
And each one seemed to say, "Hello,"
With smiles that came from down below.

We strolled along behind their bench,
And it was not the livestock stench

74

That made my stomach muscles clench,
But all those butts along the bench.

I think I am a friendly sort,
And possibly,
    a real good sport.
But how it made my guts contort
To see so many glutes distort.

I wanted to shout,
    Hoist those pants!"
To give my lunch a fighting chance.
Or maybe,
    "How 'bout underpants?"
I couldn't take a second glance.

We hurried to another space,
Potato sack or pony race,
Or just to find a happy face
Who'd wear a smile in the right place!

Idols and Icons: A Cinquain Form Debating Norm

Idols

Ideal imprints

Instantly invite eyes

Images impressed into ink

Icons

Comfort Clothes: Strands in the Sands

Here I sit,
Looking down,
As the satin waves unfold
On the wide velvet band,
Wrinkled by the lapping
Of the waves
And the breeze –
I love the beach.

At times,
I can hear the voice
Of the Master:

"Let the silken sands
Wrap your tired feet.
Fling yourself
Into the folds
Of the waters.
These are My vestments,

The fabrics of My world.
Solomon, in all his glory,
Was never so arrayed."[1]

[1] See Matthew 6:29.

Lipschtick: Simple Lines on Smile of Wine

Her smile's stuck,

Just like a clown.

A ruby guck

Is on her frown.

Forensic eyes

Might take a peek,

Then realize

It's no mystique.

For scarlet gloss

Has smeared beneath.

And, though she floss,

It's on her teeth.

Dandies on Display: A Gussied Verse to Break the Purse

Today's a holiday, and so
Our daily clothes have got to go.
We press our pants.
    Our hair we puff.
We polish shoes to strut our stuff.

And though we fancies now may feign,
Tomorrow we'll be plain again.

Loads of Laundry: Acrostic Posh on Doing Wash

Loads of laundry

Initiate insight.

Now I know:

Each ounce of energy

Needs newness.

Making mindless mounds,

Overtaking unwashed sheets

May seem mundane,

Everlasting and unnoticed.

Nevertheless, each wrinkled wonder,

Transformed to freshness,

Signals a new start.

Pinata Sonata: Swinging Toy on Party Boy

Every time,
    dressed to the nines,
Wearing all the latest lines,
He paraded,
    swarthy stride,
Felling beauties side to side.

A piñata,
    filled with sweet,
Sweeping ladies off their feet,
Seeking secrets hid within –
Everybody flocked to him.

Like a bright flamingo pink,
He lived ever on the brink:
Slightly tipsy,
    still well clad,
Noncommittal, this nomad.

Soon, this swinger got his due.
Then his whirling days were through.
This piñata, flying high,
Was struck down by passers-by.

Lovely ladies lined up long,
Each companion he'd done wrong.
Swatting strong and striking fast,
They assailed him at full blast.

When his fancy shell was tossed
And his reputation lost,
Then his dance card drew a blank,
To be absolutely frank.

But I must get this off my chest-a.
He was the life of each fiesta.

The Mirror Lied: A Rhyming Write on Altered Sight

When I was just a little girl,
I thought that I was fat.
My tiny perfect playmate
Was my only thermostat.

She had a skinny little waist
And long toothpicky limbs,
Ideal for running bases and
For climbing jungle gyms.

I had a stubby, frumpy form,
The shortest in the class –
Completely opposite to her,
The ideal hourglass.

She wore the latest fashions
With complete accessories,
And everything she tried, she did

With dignity and ease.

But I wore boyish hand-me-downs,
My brother's outgrown jeans,
Until I started earning.
Somewhere halfway through my teens.

Out by the fence,
    we'd stand a-row
To choose up sides for sport.
She'd be elected captain,
And I'd be the last resort.

And everyone adored her,
As she modeled peace and poise –
The life of every party,
She attracted all the boys.

Her phone would ring forever,
While mine held a dial tone.
She'd spend her weekends on the town,
And I'd be home alone.

I'd ponder, and I'd wonder
If my turn would come one day.
It seemed unfair
    this friend with flair
Swept everyone away.

The two of us fell out of touch
Around age seventeen.
I hit the books,
    and she went on
To be a beauty queen.

By twenty-one,
    she had three kids,
Two daughters and a son.
She caught her husband cheating,
And her world,
    it came undone.

Perhaps life was a lot more fair
Than I had ever known.

Misfortune struck her harder,
For she ended up alone.

Could be the mirror lied to us;
In hindsight, we can view.
Misjudgments and misgivings?
Gee, we never had a clue.

Reach for the Beach: A Limericked Run on a Form That Needs Sun

Hey, weatherman!
    Sound the alarm!
I don't wish to cause any harm.
But we've been locked in
For months,
    and this skin
May anyone's vision disarm.

Oh, baby.
    My feathers are riled,
My temper roused like rowdy child.
The season is ripe
To raise richer hype
And rush straight for reaches gone wild.

My limbs,
    they are paler than chalk,
Enough to make little ones squawk.

I'll waddle the sand

Until I am tanned

And issue this mantra,

"Bock-bock!"

More, More: A Ballyhoo to Overdo

Everybody wants the best;
Makes them stand out from the rest.
Man, we've gotta keep abreast,
By materials oppressed.

Fashions, furs, and fancy things –
Baubles, bangles, shiny rings.
Just like puppets,
     bound by strings,
We succumb to fortune's clings.

Gimme, gimme,
     gotta get!
Prance the shopper's pirouette.
Fill the cart up.
     Better yet,
Ratchet up the nation's debt.

Flashy car and motor boat?

Grab it.

 Make the neighbors gloat.

Social rungs are pure cutthroat;

Maybe there's no antidote.

Wave the plastic.

 Charge it all.

Let's go hit another mall.

It's a spending free-for-all.

Will we get a wake-up call?

Bills are flying everywhere.

Win the lotto, millionaire!

Lose our shirts?

 We'll not despair.

We have designer underwear.

Out of Gases and Sunglasses: Making Peace with Price Increase

I buy the cheap sunglasses,

Whatever I can find.

My cash is spent on gases,

The automotive kind.

I can't afford the fancy shades,

The pricey, hip new styles.

My car needs petrol, lowest grades,

To drive a few more miles.

I steer my wheels around the bends

And squint, so I can see.

But my generic tinted lens

Won't block the U-V-B.

I cannot justify the cost

Of sunglasses with class.

I have to pay for my exhaust.
My motor needs its gas.

Who needs to drop a hundred bucks
To polarize their sight?
We'll use C-notes to fill our trucks
And drive them just at night.

Quality Quit: Saving Chips as Style Slips

Preparing for a trip I'd take,

I chose a little browsing break.

A favorite shop

Caused me to stop,

But what I saw

    did make me quake.

No tempting

    did new styles provide;

They left no choices

    to decide,

As crooked stitch

And cheap cloth itch

Sent me off fully mystified.

Seems quality

    has hit the bricks,

As flimsy fashions fill the mix.

In shock and awe,

I quickly saw –

My closet has far better picks.

Shopping Sense: A Simple Spray on Scents at Play

While hunting about
    for a favorite scent,
A most earthy essence entwined us.
We picked up the pace
    for a quick circumvent,
But the putrid spice cloud still did find us.

"Come sample my wares,"
    cooed the clerk,
        as she bent
To refill her sprayer behind us.
"Oh, cease and desist,
    Ma'am,"
        we chanted lament,
As her sample mist nearly did blind us.

Now browsing may be,
    for a lady or gent,

A pastime to share and unwind us,

Except when a demo with active intent

And scent overdose does remind us.

Spandex and the Ex: Stylistic Throws
as Family Grows

The wedding invitation came;
His ex-wife couldn't spell my name –
Just one more way she might take aim
And try to pass decades-old blame.

His pride and joy was to be wed.
"I found the perfect dress,"
    I said.
I pulled the spandex o'er my head
And wriggled like a waterbed.

My gown, it cinched me,
    nice and tight,
Although my flesh put on a fight.
Love handles wiggled,
    left and right.
But woo-hoo!
    I looked out-a-sight.

We grabbed our gift and took our route

To prove our parenthood devout,

But dolled up like a young knock-out,

I thought I surely would pass out.

Arriving at the big to-do,

I took a panoramic view

And spotted his ex-stinkeroo,

Who chose to wear her spandex too!

Stopping Shoe Shopping: A Loose-Laced Chuckle, So I Won't Buckle

My shoe collection needs a buff;
Girls never seem to have enough.
I'd love to go the extra mile,
Kick off the season,
    step in style.

The choice today is mighty fine.
It's hard sometimes to toe the line.
Behold the sandals,
    clogs, and flats –
I'll skip the matching handbags, hats.

Those pretty slippers,
    mocs, and mules:
Oh, how to stay within the rules!
Alas, I know that I must stop.
The other shoe is sure to drop.

My footwear flies me far and wide,
Attending meetings multiplied –
To race through corridor and street,
Or anywhere I must beat feet.

No loafer, I have miles to stroll.
Would be a shame
    to scuff my sole.
My sneakers have put up a fight,
But shoestring budget ties us tight.

Still, shopping's not yet stopped,
    kaput.
The shoe is on the other foot.
His brand-new boxes still arrive,
Bright pairs that seldom see test drive.

I hope they charge not by the inch,
Although I aim not to be Grinch.
And I don't mean to drive a wedge,
So pass the polish on the ledge.

I'll brush and scrub and smooth and shine
To make old favorites mighty fine.
These Yankee hands can pinch a buck.
Just keep me from the store.
  Good luck.

Blooper-Vision: A Shiny Stint on Missing Tint

A gal I know has long been wed
To one who's known for seeing red.
Though that's not altogether true,
The story's anything but blue.

Unable to discern, perceive
The nuances with which we weave,
He's left a bit out in the dark,
Especially when he may bark.

Let's back this up and tell the tale.
Be warned: It goes beyond the pale.
This man with temper unrefined
Is absolutely color blind.

Each morning, she sets out his clothes.
The secret's out.

    Everyone knows.

When he and she have had a scratch,
His clothing doesn't seem to match.

She'll look around
    and flash a wink –
She's won.
    Just look.
    She's in the pink.
No white flag here,
    no swoop of brush.
But if he knew it, he might blush.

Stud, Sweat and Smears: When Being Brawn Is Overdrawn

A muscle man who puffs and preens
Around the fitness room's machines
Does draw attention,
    but no cheers
And nearly brings us all to tears.

He struts his stuff around the gym,
But his aroma's gross and grim.
Methinks he thinks he's power posh;
The rest of us just wish he'd wash.

Coif Duty: Tangled Talks on Ravaged Locks

They called me
    from the clipping joint.
Alright already.
    Got the point.
I sought a trim.
My roots were grim.
What master would I trust, anoint?

My mane's now
    overcooked and fried.
My wallet has
    been diced and dried.
The mirror scares.
Egads. My hairs!
At least, I can contend I tried.

I begged them
    for a slight retouch,

But it appears they did too much.

A horror flick

Might suit this chick.

But now I'm broke.

    Can we go Dutch?

Style Revival: A Rhyming Passion for Lasting Fashion

It's said that clothes can make the man,
But this I cannot understand.
If fashion sends the world a-spin,
Then I need to begin again.

My closet bulges
    at both ends,
Outdated styles,
    faded trends.
My clothing choices suit me not,
And my designers should be shot.

A finer wardrobe beckons me
That fits my person to a tee.
These gowns won't wrinkle,
    spot, or stain,
And ever stylish they'll remain.

So, Lord,

    please robe me with Your grace,

With Your eternal change of pace.

A gown of scarlet,

    washed like fleece,

Your shining glory to increase.

I need a metamorphosis,

From what I think

    to how it is.

Remove the shades

    upon my eyes,

So I can focus on the skies.

Then I will sing forevermore,

A new creation,

    to adore

Your highest mercies.

    Hear my prayer,

And life my eyes

    from things to wear.

For fashion's fickle;

    styles fail.

Your loving-kindness will prevail.

And Heaven's garment never frays,

Although we kneel to raise Your praise.

Unraveling: Nothing's As It Seams

A fashion plate or fancy dish
May not have everything she'd wish.
Beneath the buttons,
    beads, and bows
Mis-beats a heart,
    though no one knows.
Perhaps it's not about the clothes.

She'll lift her cup,
    a goblet raise,
And yet avoid another's gaze.
A polished pinky,
    long-lashed wink
May never mean
    all one might think.
She reaches for another drink.

To have one's cake and eat it too
Leaves others longing for their due.

111

All buttoned-up and tightly knit,
She zips her lip
    and grins with grit.
Perhaps they're simply not a fit.

Swimwear Is Life: A Rhymed Retort on Suits We Sport

First toddling with padded seat

To catch the items we excrete,

We graduate to ruffled skirts,

As we delight in sand and dirt.

'Ere long, we pick a racer-back

Of quick-dry nylon,

    off-the-rack.

Our bodies change,

    still teeny-weeny,

As each selects a sweet bikini.

Between our teens,

    we catch their eyes

In stretchy maillots,

    cut thigh-high.

By twenty-five,

we grow more modest
To pick a suit with tailored bodice.

We search the stores with frequent fright
To camouflage our cellulite.
The looking-glass smirks at our faces,
As we spill out in dreadful places.

So we wear gym shorts to the shore
To hide the parts that we abhor.
We stain our skin with tanning cream
To stimulate our self-esteem.

Eventually, nonetheless,
We'll don a granny swimming dress
With structured cups and girly pleats
To hide our ever-spreading seats.

Still, we feel blessed to swim at all,
To bake just like a butterball.
We tan to feel our form's improved
And call to have those moles removed.

And yet, we clamor for the rays;

We long all year for sunny rays.

Though balmy weather is our prayer,

Shopping for swimwear's our worst nightmare.

Titled, But Unbridled: A Rhythmic Reel on a Royal Ideal

There is only one bridge
    that leads in and out
Of ev'ry predicament,
    sole single route.
As terror or trial
    brings tempers to try,
She'll dodge disappointment,
    new trail to set by.

"We trudge with no grudge,
    And we beat the beasts back
That trespass the pathways
    The people must track.
And though to entitlement
    We may be born,
We fear not such privilege
    Treats us to scorn.

"Intrepid, we rise

    And select our best togs.

We follow our principles,

    Not demagogues.

Decorum may dictate

    The stroll we select.

We have to be more

    Than the people expect."

I cannot imagine

    the pressure unseen

To keep up the posture

    of princess or queen,

For she must be

    anything but Philistine.

Ah, royalty carries

    no mere in-between.

The Woes of Just-So's: Wrestling in Verse for Better or Worse

Why do we settle for things that are cheap –
For mystery burgers and panties that creep,
For cars that don't last and for colors that seep?
We purchase the worst,
    buying junk that won't keep.

The trouble has nothing to do with the tag.
The price, ever dear,
    gives us no room to brag.
To pay, we must all be halfway in the bag,
As quality flees,
    making shopping a drag.

The whiz-bang computer has gone on the fritz.
A hot, spiffy gadget is giving us fits.
But let's hit those sales with a fresh buyer's blitz.
C'mon now. Perhaps we have all lost our wits.

We'll pull out our plastic
    and frown at the bill.
We hem, and we haw,
    as we fill up the till.
But come back next week
    to revisit the thrill
Of purchasing junk
    to send off with goodwill.

Our new shoes, though stylish, sport skimpier soles.
The latest in blue jeans boast pre-shredded holes.
And yet, savvy marketers hold the controls.
How can we not notice
    for whom the bell tolls?

Mirror, Mirror: A Simple Squawk on Taking Stock

Oh, mirror, mirror, on the wall –
Do these pants make my seat look small?
Does this trim jacket bulge at all?
And am I in for fashion's fall?

Sometimes a body must assess.
We check the looking-glass to dress –
Might even fuss,
    I do confess.
I've taken this one to excess.

Eventually, we may find
We grow less to the glass confined
And care not of the eyes unkind
Who may be pettily inclined.

We cinch our sashes,
    tuck each cuff,

Ignoring expert fashion buff.

"Back off," we cry.

    "Enough's enough,"

And step outside in shoes with scuffs.

For life is in the roundabout.

It's not tied up in clothing's clout.

Though some may pick and peck and pout,

The victory's in breaking out.

Worn Out Without a Doubt: Poetic Talk on Taking Stock

Abandonment is agony.

Desertion's an epiphany.

My favorite rags,

    I must release.

Disbanded duds

    have lost their lease.

Here lies what's left

    of my best shirt –

Relinquished,

    threadbare,

      soiled with dirt.

I left it in the wash too long,

And now it's sung

    its own swan song.

This comfy top,

    beyond the sew,

Is fit now just to scare a crow.

Farewell, old friend, you've done your due.

It's time to prove another true.

No Worse for Wear: A Patterned Wheel, Life to Reveal

A little girl sat down to sew –
No notion what she did not know.
She learned to tuck and pleat and baste
And never did a remnant waste.

With pins and thimble,
    style began.
Throughout her years,
    this thread it ran.
She'd sit,
    duet with Singer's song,
Delighting in her craft lifelong.

From yardages of wovens, knits,
She undertook her fashion blitz.
And whether it be play or prom,
She'd fashion garb to beat the bomb.

Thus, handily while still in youth,
She ironed out the simple truth:
No spending renders one well-bred,
Ten-dollar hat on five-cent head.

Home-sewn from scraps or ready-made,
Mere clothing does not make the grade.
The secret is to find delight
In what we do with all our might.

When she shall reach her final stitch,
The pattern she may seek to switch.
Her hands and eyes already cramp,
But none can dim her inner lamp.

As silver threads weave through her hair,
She surely is no worse for wear.

About the author

Linda Ann Nickerson is a confessed frequent fashion victim, but she has lived to tell the tales and even laugh at them.

An award-winning poet and former public relations executive, she writes news and features for several well-known websites – when she's not penning poetry, weaving stories, riding horses, running tandem canicross, trail biking, or training for her next marathon.

Additional books from Linda Ann Nickerson include:

- *25 Top Tips for Promoting Your Equestrian Event: Get the Herd Out*
- *Absent Nightmare Zinnias: Rhymed Acrostics from A to Z*
- *Equine Reveries: Do Horse Dreams Pack Deeper Meanings?*
- *Horseplay Secrets: Learning in Rhyme from Equines Sublime*
- *How to Write a Book Review in 10 Easy Steps*
- *Stealing Wonder: A Rhyming Race to Capture Grace*
- *That's a Wrap: A Story of Grace in a Most Special Place*
- *What's in Santa's Sleigh This Christmas?*